NINJA
IN ACTION!

by Beth Davies

Editor Beth Davies
Designer Sam Bartlett
Pre-production Producer Siu Yin Chan
Producer Sarah Burke
Managing Editor Paula Regan
Design Manager Jo Connor
Publisher Julie Ferris
Art Director Lisa Lanzarini
Publishing Director Simon Beecroft

Reading Consultant Linda B. Gambrell, Ph.D

First American Edition, 2018
Published in the United States by DK Publishing
345 Hudson Street, New York, New York 10014

Page design copyright © 2018 Dorling Kindersley Limited
DK, a Division of Penguin Random House LLC
18 19 20 21 22 10 9 8 7 6 5 4 3 2 1
001–307126–Jan/2018

A catalog record for this book is available from the Library of Congress.

ISBN: 978-1-4654-6658-7 (Paperback)
ISBN: 978-1-4654-6659-4 (Hardcover)

DK books are available at special discounts when purchased in bulk for sales promotions,
premiums, fund-raising, or educational use. For details, contact: DK Publishing
SpecialMarkets, 345 Hudson Street, New York, New York 10014
SpecialSales@dk.com

Printed and bound in China.

A WORLD OF IDEAS:
SEE ALL THERE IS TO KNOW

www.dk.com
www.LEGO.com

Contents

The ninja

These six ninja
are brave heroes.
They protect their
home, Ninjago City.
Master Wu is their
wise teacher.

Lloyd

Jay

Nya

Zane

Cole

Master Wu

Kai

Dragon flight

The ninja have lots of ways
to travel.

Each ninja has their own
dragon to ride.

Green Ninja Lloyd flies
a green dragon.

Fire Ninja Kai and Water Ninja
Nya are brother and sister.
They share a two-headed
dragon.

Up in the air

Lloyd has a flying vehicle.
It is called *Destiny's Shadow*.
It can also float on water.
Master Wu flies in his
hot-air balloon.
Earth Ninja Cole flies a plane.
It fires missiles at top speed.

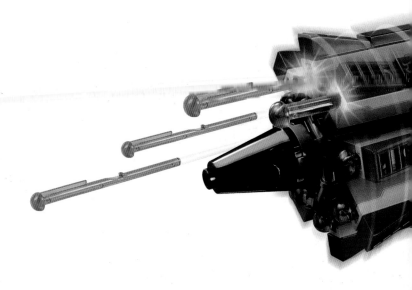

Enemy vehicles

There are many villains
in Ninjago City!
They drive strange vehicles.

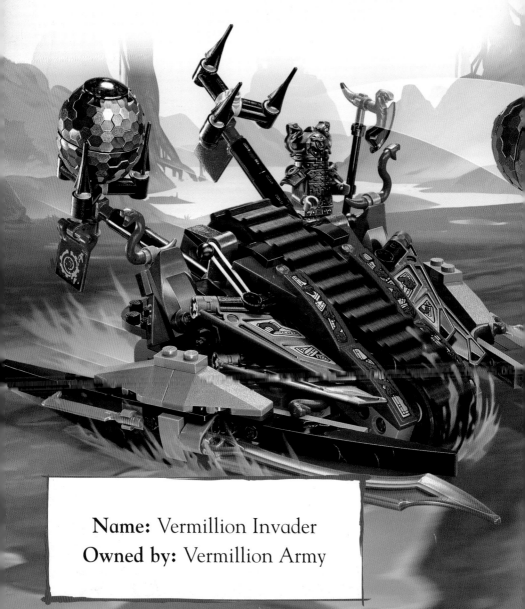

Name: Vermillion Invader
Owned by: Vermillion Army

Name:
Morro Dragon

Owned by:
Ghost Army

Name:
Raid Zeppelin

Owned by:
Sky Pirates

Name:
Anacondrai Crusher

Owned by:
Anacondrai

Bike chase

The ninja ride fast bikes.
They are ready to catch
speedy enemies.
Kai and Nya race each other.
Jay is the Lightning Ninja.
He is as quick as a flash on
his bright blue bike.

Cave base

The ninja's vehicles are stored in a cave.

The ninja must keep them safe!

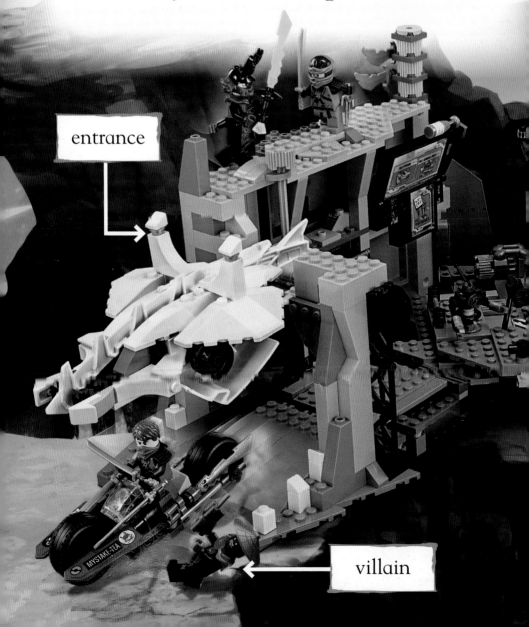

entrance

villain

Nya

snake

Master Wu

storage area

On the road

Ninja need powerful vehicles for their battles.
Ice Ninja Zane is a robot.
His vehicle has strong armor.

Cole's car has four big wheels.
It can race across bumpy land.
When the car stops, Cole leaps
into action.

Mech battles

Mechs are special vehicles that look like robots. The mechs have many weapons and gadgets.

The ninja stand inside
the mechs to control them.
Can you see Jay and
Zane in their mechs?

Samurai X

The ninja are not the only
heroes in Ninjago City.
Samurai X is a brave warrior.
Nya has built Samurai X
a special vehicle.
Now the heroes can
work together!

Quiz

1. Which element is Cole the Ninja of?

2. Which group of villains flies the Raid Zeppelin?

3. Who is this wise teacher?

4. Which two ninja share a dragon?

5. What type of vehicle is this?

Index

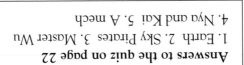

Answers to the quiz on page 22
1. Earth 2. Sky Pirates 3. Master Wu
4. Nya and Kai 5. A mech

23

A LEVEL FOR EVERY READER

This book is a part of an exciting four-level reading series to support children in developing the habit of reading widely for both pleasure and information. Each book is designed to develop a child's reading skills, fluency, grammar awareness, and comprehension in order to build confidence and enjoyment when reading.

Ready for a Level 1 (Learning to Read) book
A child should:
- be familiar with most letters and sounds.
- understand how to blend sounds together to make words.
- have an awareness of syllables and rhyming sounds.

A valuable and shared reading experience
For many children, learning to read requires much effort, but adult participation can make reading both fun and easier. Here are a few tips on how to use this book with an early reader:

Check out the contents together:
- tell the child the book title and talk about what the book might be about.
- read about the book on the back cover and talk about the contents page to help heighten interest and expectation.
- chat about the pictures on each page.
- discuss new or difficult words.

Support the reader:
- give the book to the young reader to turn the pages.
- if the book seems too hard, support the child by sharing the reading task.

Talk at the end of each page:
- ask questions about the text and the meaning of the words used—this helps develop comprehension skills.
- read the quiz at the end of the book and encourage the reader to answer the questions, if necessary, by turning back to the relevant pages to find the answers.

Series consultant, Dr. Linda Gambrell, Distinguished Professor of Education at Clemson University, has served as President of the National Reading Conference, the College Reading Association, and the International Reading Association.